SCIENTOLOGY
Improving Life in a Troubled World

Founded and developed by L. Ron Hubbard, Scientology is an applied religious philosophy which offers an exact route through which anyone can regain the truth and simplicity of his spiritual self.

Scientology consists of specific axioms that define the underlying causes and principles of existence and a vast area of observations in the humanities, a philosophic body that literally applies to the entirety of life.

This broad body of knowledge resulted in two applications of the subject: first, a technology for man to increase his spiritual awareness and attain the freedom sought by many great philosophic teachings; and, second, a great number of fundamental principles men can use to improve their lives. In fact, in this second application, Scientology offers nothing less than practical methods to better *every* aspect of our existence—means to create new ways of life. And from this comes the subject matter you are about to read.

Compiled from the writings of L. Ron Hubbard, the data presented here is but one of the tools which can be found in *The Scientology Handbook*. A comprehensive guide, the handbook contains numerous applications of Scientology which can be used to improve many other areas of life.

In this booklet, the editors have augmented the data with a short introduction, practical exercises and examples of successful application.

Courses to increase your understanding and further materials to broaden your knowledge are available at your nearest Scientology church or mission, listed at the back of this booklet.

Many new phenomena about man and life are described in Scientology, and so you may encounter terms in these pages you are not familiar with. These are described the first time they appear and in the glossary at the back of the booklet.

Scientology is for use. It is a practical philosophy, something one *does*. Using this data, you *can* change conditions.

Millions of people who want to do something about the conditions they see around them have applied this knowledge. They know that life can be improved. And they know that Scientology works.

Use what you read in these pages to help yourself and others and you will too.

CHURCH OF SCIENTOLOGY INTERNATIONAL

*P*lummeting productivity, massive layoffs, sour relations between management and labor, executive incompetence and dishonest business dealings all plague the workplace. It is small wonder that the act of work is a source of stress and anxiety for millions.

How to increase job efficiency and productivity, how to handle upsets and confusion in the workplace and how to overcome exhaustion are all matters that concern both the laborer and the manager. Their resolution would bring about not only greater security but greater satisfaction.

This booklet contains some of the wide array of principles and techniques L. Ron Hubbard developed for application in the workplace. Work not only **can** be both rewarding and fulfilling, but as the major activity in most of our lives, it **should** be. Utilization of this information will help you make it just that.

HANDLING CONFUSION IN THE WORKPLACE

One might be led to believe there was something confusing about navigating one's career in the world of work. And confusion there is, to one who is not equipped with guides and maps.

As one looks at the many factors which might derange his life and undermine his security, the impression is, confusion seems well founded and it can be said with truth that all difficulties are fundamentally confusions. Given enough menace, enough unknown, a man ducks his head and tries to swing through it blindly. He has been overcome by confusions.

Enough unsolved problems add up to a huge confusion. Every now and then, on his job, enough conflicting orders bring the worker into a state of confusion. A modern plant can be so poorly managed that the entire thing appears to be a vast confusion to which no answer is possible.

Luck is the usual answer one resorts to in a confusion. If the forces about one seem too great, one can always "rely on his luck." By luck we mean "destiny not personally guided." When one turns loose of an automobile wheel and hopes the car will stay on the road by luck, he is often disappointed. And so it is in life. Those things left to chance become less likely to work themselves out. One has seen a friend shutting his eyes to the bill collectors and gritting his teeth while he hopes that he will win at the races and solve all his problems. One has known people who handled their lives this way for years. Indeed, one of English novelist Charles Dickens' great characters had the entire philosophy of "waiting for something to turn up." But luck, while we grant that it *is* a potent element, is only necessary amid a strong current of confusing factors. If one has to have *luck* to see him through, then it follows that one isn't any longer at his own automobile wheel and it follows, too, that one is dealing with a confusion.

It would be wise, then, to understand exactly what a confusion is and how it could be resolved.

Confusion and the Stable Datum

A confusion can be defined as any set of factors or circumstances which do not seem to have any immediate solution. More broadly, a confusion is *random motion*.

If you were to stand in heavy traffic you would be likely to feel confused by all the motion whizzing around you. If you were to stand in a heavy storm, with leaves and papers flying by, you would be likely to be confused.

Is it possible to actually understand a confusion? Is there any such thing as an "anatomy of confusion"? Yes, there is.

If, as a switchboard operator, you had ten calls hitting your board at once, you might feel confused. But is there any answer to the situation? If, as a shop foreman, you have three emergencies and an accident all at the same time, you might feel confused. But is there any answer to that?

A confusion is only a confusion so long as *all* particles are in motion. A confusion is only a confusion so long as no factor is clearly defined or understood.

Confusion is the basic cause of stupidity. To the stupid all things except the very simple ones are confused. Thus if one knew the anatomy of confusion, no matter how bright one might be, he would be brighter.

If you have ever had to teach some ambitious young person who was not too bright, you will understand this well. You attempt to explain how such and so works. You go over it and over it and over it. And then you turn him loose and he promptly makes a complete botch of it. He "didn't understand," he "didn't grasp it." You can simplify your understanding of his misunderstanding by saying, very rightly, "He was confused."

Ninety-nine percent of all education fails, when it fails, on the grounds that the student was confused.

And not only in the realm of the job, but in life itself, when failure approaches, it is born, one way or another, from confusion. To learn of machinery or to live life, one has to be able either to stand up to confusion or to take it apart.

We have in Scientology a certain doctrine (principle) about confusion. It is called the *Doctrine of the Stable Datum*.

If you saw a great many pieces of paper whirling about a room they would look confused until you picked out *one* piece of paper to be the piece of paper by which everything else was in motion. In other words, a confusing motion can be understood by conceiving one thing to be motionless.

In a stream of traffic all would be confusion unless you were to conceive one car to be motionless in relation to the other cars and so to see others in relation to the one.

The switchboard operator receiving ten calls at once solves the confusion by labeling, correctly or incorrectly, one call as the first call to receive her attention. The confusion of ten calls all at once becomes less confusing the moment she singles out one call to be answered. The shop foreman confronted by three emergencies and an accident needs only to elect his *first* target of attention to start the cycle of bringing about order again.

Until one selects *one* datum, *one* factor, *one* particular in a confusion of particles, the confusion continues. The *one* thing selected and used becomes the *stable datum* for the remainder.

Any body of knowledge, more particularly and exactly, is built from *one datum*. That is its *stable datum*. Invalidate it and the entire body of knowledge falls apart. A stable datum does not have to be the correct one. It is simply the one that keeps things from being in a confusion and on which others are aligned.

Now, in teaching an ambitious young man to use a machine, he failed to grasp your directions, if he did, because he lacked a stable datum.

A confusion exists when <u>all</u> particles are in motion.

It becomes less confusing when <u>one</u> item is singled out and becomes the stable datum for the remainder.

6

One fact had to be brought home to him first. Grasping that, he could grasp others. One is stupid, then, or confused in any confusing situation until he has fully grasped *one fact* or one item.

Confusions, no matter how big and hard to overcome they may seem, are composed of data or factors or particles. They have pieces. Grasp one piece and locate it thoroughly. Then see how the others function in relation to it and you have steadied the confusion and, relating other things to what you have grasped, you will soon have mastered the confusion in its entirety.

In teaching a boy to run a machine, don't throw a torrent of data at him and then point out his errors: that's confusion to him, that makes him respond stupidly. Find some entrance point to his confusion, *one datum*. Tell him, "This is a machine." It may be that all the directions were flung at someone who had no real certainty, no real order of existence. "This is a machine," you say. Then make him sure of it. Make him feel it, fiddle with it, push at it. "This is a machine," tell him. And you'd be surprised how long it may take, but you'd be surprised as well how his certainty increases. Out of all the complexities he must learn to operate it, he must know *one datum* first. It is not even important *which* datum he first learns well, beyond that it is better to teach him a *simple basic datum.* You can show him what it does, you can explain to him the final product, you can tell him why *he* has been selected to run this machine. *But* you *must* make one basic datum clear to him or else he will be lost in confusion.

Confusion is uncertainty. Confusion is stupidity. Confusion is insecurity. When you think of uncertainty, stupidity and insecurity, think of confusion and you'll have it down pat.

What, then, is certainty? Lack of confusion. What then is intelligence? Ability to handle confusion. What then is security? The ability to go through or around or to bring order to confusion. Certainty, intelligence and security are lack of, or ability to handle, confusion.

How does luck fit into confusion? Luck is the hope that some uncontrolled chance will get one through. Counting on luck is an abandonment of control. That's apathy.

Control and Confusion

There is *good* control and *bad* control. The difference between them is certainty and uncertainty. Good control is certain, positive, predictable. Bad control is uncertain, variable and unpredictable. With good control one can be certain, with bad control one is never certain. A foreman who makes a rule effective today but not tomorrow, who makes George obey but not James, is exercising bad control; in that foreman's wake will come uncertainty and insecurity, no matter what his personal attributes may be.

Because there can be so much uncertain, stupid control, some of us begin to believe that all control is bad. But this is very far from true. Control is necessary if one would bring any order into confusions. One must be able to control things, his body, his thoughts, at least to some degree, to do anything whatever.

A confusion could be called an *uncontrolled randomness*. Only those who can exert some control over that randomness can handle confusions. Those who cannot exert control actually breed confusions.

The difference between good and bad control then becomes more obvious. The difference between good and bad here is *degree*. A thorough, positive control can be predicted by others. Therefore it is good control. A nonpositive, sloppy control cannot be predicted; therefore it is a bad control. Intention also has something to do with control. Control can be used for constructive purposes or destructive purposes; but you will discover that when destructive purposes are *intended*, bad control is used.

Thus there is a great deal to this entire subject of *confusion*. You may find it rather odd for confusion itself to be used here as a target. But you will find that it is an excellent common denominator to all that we consider evil in life. And if one can become master of confusions, his attention is freed for constructive activity. So long as one is being confused by confusions, all he can think about are destructive things—what he wants to do most is to destroy the confusion.

So let us then learn first how to destroy confusions. And this, we find, is a rather simple thing. When *all* particles seem to be in motion, halt one and see how the others move according to it and then you will find less confusion present. With one adopted as a *stable datum* others can be made to fall in line. Thus an emergency, a machine, a job or life itself can be viewed and understood and one can be free.

Let us take a glance at how this works. There are a number of things which might influence obtaining, holding and improving a job. One can handle this entire problem, as people most often do, by entering into the problem the single datum, "I can get and hold a job." By clutching to this as a single belief, the confusions and insecurities of life become less effective, less confusing.

But suppose one has done this: Suppose that without further investigating the problem, one, when young, gritted his teeth and shut his eyes and said, "I can get and hold a job, come what may. Therefore I am not going to worry about the economics of existence anymore." Well, that was fine.

Later on, without warning, one got fired. One was out of work for ten weeks. He felt then, even when he did get a new job, less secure, less confident. And let us say that some accident occurred and one was out of a job again. When once more unemployed, he was once more even less confident, less secure. Why?

Let us take a look at the opposite side of this Doctrine of the Stable Datum. If we do, we learn that confusions are held ineffective by stable data and that, when the stable datum is shaken, the confusion comes into being again.

Let us envision a confusion as stopped. It is still scattered but it is stopped. What stopped it? The adoption of a stable datum. Let us say that one was bothered badly in the home by a mother-in-law. One day, after a quarrel, one stalked out and by inspiration said to himself, "All mothers-in-law are evil." That was a decision. That, rightly or wrongly, was a stable datum adopted in a confusion. At once one felt better. He could deal with or live with the problem now. He knew that "all mothers-in-law" were evil. It wasn't true, but it was a stable datum. Then one day, when he was in trouble, his mother-in-law stepped forward, unwaveringly loyal, and paid not only the rent but the other debt, too. At once he felt very confused. This act of kindness should not have been a thing to bring in confusion. After all, hadn't she solved the problem? Then why does one feel upset about it? *Because the stable datum has been shaken.* The entire confusion of the past problem came into action again by reason of the demonstrated falsity of the stable datum.

To make anyone confused, all you have to do is locate their stable data and invalidate them. By criticism or proof it is only necessary to shake these few stable data to get all a person's confusions back into action.

You see, stable data do not have to be true. They are simply adopted. When adopted, then one looks at other data in relation to them. Thus the adoption of *any* stable datum will tend to nullify the confusion addressed. *But* if that stable datum is shaken, invalidated, disproven, then one is left again with the confusion. Of course, all one has to do is adopt a new stable datum or put the old stable datum back in place, but he'd have to know Scientology in order to accomplish this smoothly.

Let us say one has no fears of national economy because of a heroic political figure who is trying his best. That man is the stable datum to all one's confusions about national economy. Thus one "isn't worried." But one day circumstances or his political enemies shake him as a datum. They "prove" he was really dishonest. One then becomes worried all over again about national economy. Maybe you adopted some philosophy because the speaker seemed such a pleasant chap. Then some person carefully proves to you that the speaker was actually a thief or worse. One adopted the philosophy because one needed some peace from his thoughts. Invalidating the speaker would then at once bring back the confusion one faced originally.

All right. We looked at the confusion of the workaday world when we were young and we held it all back by stating grimly, "I can get and keep a job." That was the stable datum. We did get a job. But we got fired. The confusion of the workaday world then became very confusing. If we have only the one stable datum, "I can get and keep a job," then, assuredly, one is going to spend some confusing periods in his working life. A far, far better stable datum would be, "I understand about life and jobs. Therefore I can get, hold and improve them."

Confusion need not be an unavoidable and persistent part of one's working life. By employing the Doctrine of the Stable Datum one can gradually bring order and understanding to any situation.

REACH AND WITHDRAW

With an understanding of confusion and the need for good control to bring order, one can easily observe workers and executives who breed confusions with bad control. There is a very simple but extremely powerful method to get a person familiarized and in communication with things so that he can be more in control of them. This is called Reach and Withdraw.

One would not expect a person to have much control or understanding of or skill in something with which he was not familiar.

The keynote of familiarity is communication.

A person is out of communication with something because he is withdrawing from it and is not about to reach out to or contact any part of it.

If a person cannot reach and withdraw from a thing, he will be the effect of that thing.

If a person can reach for something and withdraw from it, he could be said to be in communication with that thing.

To be in communication with something is to be in a more causative position in relation to it.

By REACH we mean touching or taking hold of. It is defined as "to get to," "come to" and/or "arrive at."

By WITHDRAW we mean move back from, let go.

The Reach and Withdraw procedure brings a person into communication with and into a more causative position in relation to objects, people, spaces, boundaries and situations.

In the physical universe, communication with objects, forms, spaces and boundaries is best established by actual physical contact.

Reach and Withdraw is a valuable tool to use to get a person into good communication with his work environment, especially the tools and objects he uses.

A pilot would do Reach and Withdraw on all the objects and spaces of his airplane, his hangar, the earth; a secretary would do Reach and Withdraw on her typewriter, her chair, walls, spaces, her desk, etc.

Feeling comfortable with the tools of one's trade is a very important step in getting out products. One can increase the amount of production tremendously with this action.

For example, a flight surgeon who was trained in this procedure used Reach and Withdraw on his squadron and for one whole year there was not one single accident, not even so much as the touch of a wing tip to a wing tip. It is probably the only squadron in history that went a whole year without even a minor accident.

Procedure

Reach and Withdraw procedure is easily learned. It can be done on any object or area. It can be done on an individual's job environment, on a new piece of equipment, a machine, anything. It is done until the person is in good communication with his general environment or specific area being addressed.

1. Take the person to the area where you will be doing Reach and Withdraw. Explain to him you are going to do Reach and Withdraw and explain the procedure.

2. Tell him the commands to be used and ensure he understands these. The commands are:

A. "Reach that _____." (naming and pointing to an object or person or area)

B. "Withdraw from that _____." (naming and pointing to the same object or person or area)

A thing or part of something (e.g., "the big red button on the front of the machine") or a space or a person is named in the blank.

3. Give him the first command. For example, "Reach that big red button on the front of the machine."

Always point to the object (or person, space, etc.) each time you give a command so there will be no mistake made by the person doing it.

4. When the person has carried out the command, acknowledge him by saying "Thank you," or "Good," etc.

5. Now give the second command, "Withdraw from that big red button on the front of the machine." Acknowledge him when he has done so.

6. Continue to alternate the commands A, B, A, B and so on, with an acknowledgment after the execution of each command, having the person touch different parts of the object or area.

7. Reach and withdraw from that one thing, space or person until the individual either has a minor win, or until three consecutive sets of commands have been executed with no change in the person's motions or attitude. By "minor win" is meant a small improvement for the person, such as his feeling a bit better about the object or area, or simply experiencing an increased feeling of well-being.

8. Next, another object, space or person is chosen and the commands are taken to a win on that item.

Don't keep the person reaching and withdrawing endlessly from the same *part* of anything that is being used but go to different points and parts of an object being touched.

Walk around with the person doing the action, ensuring that he actually does get in physical contact with the points or areas of objects, spaces or people.

Choose objects in such a way as to progress from smaller objects to the larger objects available, touching different parts of each one in turn to a minor win of some sort on that object or three sets of commands with no change. Also include walls and floors and other parts of the environment in doing this procedure.

When doing the action on a space or a room rather than an object, have the person walk into the room and walk out of the room over and over.

9. Continue until the person has a major win or a good realization and is very happy about the whole area being addressed. A major win would be a large improvement for the person such as a new awareness of his work area or a certainty about his job. Reach and Withdraw would not be continued past such a point.

Reach and Withdraw on the objects, people, situations, spaces and boundaries of a person's job will greatly assist his control, familiarity and understanding of it.

Reach and Withdraw is done by having a person reach for and withdraw from things in the environment.

REACH

WITHDRAW

As the person reaches and withdraws from the objects, walls, floors and other parts of the environment...

...his control, familiarity and understanding of it can increase greatly.

HANDLING EXHAUSTION IN THE WORKADAY WORLD

To work or not to work, that is the question. The answer to that question in most men's minds is exhaustion.

One begins to feel, after he has been long on a job and has been considerably abused on that job, that to work any more would be quite beyond his endurance. He is tired. The thought of doing certain things makes him tired. He thinks of raising his energy or of being able to force his way along just a little bit further, and if he does so he is thinking in the wrong channels since the answer to exhaustion has little if anything to do with energy.

Exhaustion is a very important subject, not only to an individual involved in earning his own living but to the state as well.

Scientology has rather completely established the fact that the downfall of the individual begins when he is no longer able to work. All it is necessary to do to degrade or upset an individual is to prevent him from working. Even the police have now come to recognize the basic Scientology principle that the primary thing wrong with a criminal is that he cannot work, and police have begun to look for this factor in an individual in establishing his criminality.

The subject of exhaustion is also the subject of prevented work. In the case of soldiers and sailors hospitalized during war, it is found that a few months in the hospital tends to break the morale of the soldier or sailor to such a point that he may become a questionable asset when returned to his service. This is not necessarily the result of his lowered abilities. It is the result of injury compounded by inactivity. A soldier who is wounded and cared for in a field hospital close to the front and is returned to duty the moment he can possibly support such duties will be found to retain, in a large measure, his morale. Of course the injury received has a tendency to repel him from the level of action which he once thought best but, even so, he is in better shape than a soldier who is sent to a hospital in the rear. The soldier who is sent to the hospital in the rear is being told, according to his viewpoint, that he is not particularly necessary to the war. Without actually adding up these principles, the word *exhaustion* began a general use coupled with neurosis. This was based on the fact that people with a neurosis simply looked exhausted. There was no more coordination to it than that. Actually, a person who has been denied the right to work, particularly one who has been injured and then denied the right to work, will eventually encounter exhaustion.

It has been discovered that there is no such thing as gradual diminishing by continuing contact of the energy of the individual. One does not become exhausted simply because one has worked too long or too hard. One becomes exhausted when he has worked sufficiently long to reactivate the pain and emotion of a past bad memory of some old injury.

One of the characteristics of this injury will be exhaustion. Chronic exhaustion, then, is not the product of long hours and arduous application. It is the product of the accumulation of the shocks and injuries incident to life, each of them perhaps only a few seconds or a few hours long and adding up perhaps to a totality of only fifty or seventy-five hours. But this accumulation—the accumulation of injury, repulsion and shock—eventually mounts up to a complete inability to do anything.

Exhaustion can then be trained into a person by refusing to allow him as a child to have any part in the society, or it can be beaten into a person by the various injuries or shocks he may receive incident to his particular activities. Clear up either of these two points and you have cleared up exhaustion.

Exhaustion, then, is actually the subject of a trained Scientology practitioner since only a Scientologist can adequately handle it.

There is a point, however, which is below exhaustion. This is the point of not knowing when one is tired. An individual can become a sort of hectic puppet that goes on working and working without even realizing that he is working at all, and suddenly collapses from a tiredness he was not experiencing.

Here the individual has failed to control things. Eventually he is incapable of handling anything even resembling tools of the trade or an environment of work and so is unable to inhabit such an environment or handle such tools. The individual can then have many hard words cast in his direction. He can be called lazy, he can be called a bum, he can be called criminal. But the truth of the matter is he is no more capable of righting his own condition without expert help than he is capable of diving to the center of the earth.

There are, however, some means of recovering one's energy and enthusiasm for work short of consultation with a Scientology practitioner. These are relatively simple and very easy to understand.

Extroversion and Introversion

Introversion is a simple thing. It means looking in too closely. And extroversion is also a simple thing. It means nothing more than being able to look outward.

It could be said that there are introverted personalities and extroverted personalities. An extroverted personality is one who is capable of looking around the environment. An introverted personality is only capable of looking inward at himself.

A person who is capable of looking at the world around him and seeing it quite real and quite bright is, of course, in a state of extroversion. He can look out, in other words. He can also work. He can also see situations and handle and control those things which he has to handle and control, and can stand by and watch those things which he does not have to control and be interested in them therefore.

The person who is introverted is a person who has probably passed exhaustion some way back. He has had his attention focused closer and closer to him (basically by old injuries which are still capable of exerting their influence upon him) until he is actually looking inward and not outward. He is shying away from solid objects. He does not see a reality in other people and things around him.

Now let us take the actual subject of work. Work is the application of attention and action to people or objects located in space.

When one is no longer able to face people or objects or the space in which they are located without flinching or avoiding, he begins to have a lost feeling. He begins to move in a mistiness. Things are not real to him and he is relatively incapable of controlling those things around him. He has accidents. He has bad luck. He has things turn against him simply because he is not handling them or controlling them or even observing them correctly. The future to him seems very bad, so bad sometimes that he cannot face it. This person could be said to be severely introverted.

In work his attention is riveted on objects which are usually at the most only a few feet from him. He pays his closest attention to articles which are within the reach of his hands. This puts his attention away from extroversion at least to some spot in focus in front of his face. His attention fixes there. If this is coincident with some old injury incident or operation, he is likely to fix his attention as well on some spot in former times and reactivates some past bad memory so that he gets the pains and ills and the feeling of tiredness or apathy or subapathy which he had during that moment of injury. As his attention is continuously riveted there he of course has a tendency to look only there, even when he is not working.

Let us take an accountant. An accountant's eyes are on books at fixed distances from his eyes. At length he becomes "shortsighted." Actually he doesn't become shortsighted, he becomes book-sighted. His eyes most easily fix on a certain point in distance. Now as he fixes his attention there he tends to withdraw even from that point until at length he does not quite reach even his own books. Then he is fitted with glasses so that he can see the books more clearly. His vision and his attention are much the same thing.

A person who has a machine or books or objects continually at a fixed distance from him leaves his work and tends to keep his attention fixed exactly where his work was. In other words, his attention never really leaves his work at all. Although he goes home he is still really sitting in the office. His attention is still fixed on the environment of his work. If this environment is coincident with some injury or accident (and who does not have one of these at least?), he begins to feel weariness or tiredness.

Is there a cure for this?

Of course, only a trained Scientology practitioner could clear up this difficulty entirely. But the worker does have something which he can do.

Now here is the wrong thing to do, regardless of whether one is a bookkeeper, an accountant, a clerk, an executive or a machinist. The wrong thing to do is to leave work, go home, sit down and fix attention on an object more or less at the same distance from one as one confronts continually at work. In the case of a foreman, for instance, who is continually talking to men at a certain distance away from him, the wrong thing for him to do is to go home and talk to his wife at the same distance. The next thing she knows, she will be getting orders just as though she were a member of the shop. Definitely the wrong thing to do is to go home and sit down and read a paper, eat some dinner and go to bed. If a man practiced the routine of working all day and then sitting down "to rest" with a book or a newspaper in the evening, it is certain that sooner or later he would start to feel quite exhausted and then after a while would fall even below that and would not even wonder at his unwillingness to perform tasks which were once very easy to him.

Is there a right thing to do? Yes, there is. An individual who is continually fixed upon some object of work should fix his attention otherwise after working hours.

Take a Walk

There is a Scientology procedure known as "Take a Walk." This procedure is very easy to perform. When one feels tired on finishing his work, no matter if the thought of doing so is almost all that he can tolerate without falling through the floor, he should go out and walk around the block until he feels rested. In short, he should walk around the block and look at things until he sees the things he is walking near. It does not matter how many times he walked around the block, he should walk around the block until he feels better.

In doing this it will be found that one will become a little brighter at first and then will become very much more tired. He will become sufficiently tired that he knows now that he should go to bed and have a good night's sleep. This is not the time to stop walking since he is walking through exhaustion. He is walking out his exhaustion. He is not handling the exhaustion by physical exercise. The physical exercise has always appeared to be the more important factor to people, but the exercise is relatively unimportant. The factor that is important is the unfixing of his attention from his work to the material world in which he is living.

When one is so tired that he can barely drag himself around, or is so tired that he is hectically unable to rest at all, it is actually necessary that he confront masses. It is even doubtful if there is such a thing as a "fall of physical energy." Naturally there is a limit to this procedure. One cannot work all day and walk around the block all night and go to work the next day again and still expect to feel relieved. But one should certainly spend some time extroverting after having introverted all day.

"Take a Walk" is, within reason, a near cure-all. If one feels antagonistic toward one's wife, the wrong thing to do is to beat her. The right thing to do is to go out and take a walk around the block until one feels better, and make her walk around the block in the opposite direction until an extroversion from the situation is achieved. It will be discovered that all domestic quarrels, particularly amongst working people, stem from the fact that, having been overfixed (rather than

A simple remedy for exhaustion is "Take a Walk." A person simply walks around the block and looks at things.

As one continues to walk around the block and look at things . . .

. . . feelings of exhaustion can vanish, making the person feel more energetic.

overstrained) on one's work and the situations connected with it, one has failed to control certain things in his working environment. He then comes home and seeks to find something he *can* control. This is usually the marital partner or the children, and when one fails even there he is apt to worsen with a vengeance.

The extroversion of attention is as necessary as the work itself. There is nothing really wrong with introverting attention or with work. If one didn't have something to be interested in, he would go to pieces entirely. But if one works, it will be found that an unnatural tiredness is apt to set in. When this is found to be the case then the answer to this is not a drop into unconsciousness for a few hours as in sleep, but in actually extroverting the attention and then getting a really relaxing sleep.

These principles of extroversion and introversion have many ramifications and, although "Take a Walk" is almost laughable in its simplicity, there are many more complicated Scientology procedures in case one wished to get more complicated. However, in the main, "Take a Walk" will take care of an enormous number of difficulties attendant to work. Remember that when doing it one will get more tired at first and will then get fresher. This phenomenon has been noted by athletes. It is called the second wind. The second wind is really getting enough environment and enough mass in order to run out the exhaustion of the last race. There is no such thing as a second wind. There *is* such a thing as a return to extroversion on the physical world in which one lives.

Look Them Over

Similar to "Take a Walk" is another procedure known as "Look Them Over." If one has been talking to people all day, has been selling people all day or has been handling people who are difficult to handle all day, the wrong thing to do is to run away from all the people there are in the world. You see, the person who gets over-strained when handling people has had large difficulties with people. He has perhaps been operated upon by doctors, and the half-seen vision of them standing around the operating table identifies all people with doctors; that is to say, all people who stand still. This, by the way, is one of the reasons why doctors become so thoroughly hated in a society since they do insist on practices known as surgery and anesthesia and such incidents become interlocked with everyday incidents.

Exhaustion because of contact with people is due to one's attention having been fixated upon certain people while his attention, he felt, ought to be on other people. This straining of attention has actually cut down the number of people that he was observing.

The cure for this is a very simple one. One should go to a place that is very well populated such as a railroad station or a main street and should simply walk along the street noting people. Simply look at people—that is all. It will be found after a while that one feels people aren't so bad and one has a much kinder attitude toward them and, more importantly, the job condition of becoming overstrained with people tends to go away if one makes a practice of doing this every late afternoon for a few weeks.

This is one of the smartest things that a salesman can do, since a salesman, above and beyond others, has a vested interest in being able to handle people and get them to do exactly what he wants them to do, that is, buy what he has to sell. As he fixes his attention on just one too many customers, he gets tired of the whole idea of talking to people or selling and drops down to lower emotional levels in all of his activities and operations and begins to consider himself all kinds of a swindler and at length doesn't consider himself anything at all. He, like the others, should simply find populated places and walk along looking at people. He will find after a while that people really do exist and that they aren't so bad. One of the things that happens to people in high government is that they are being continually "protected from" the people and they at length become quite disgusted with the whole subject and are apt to do all manner of strange things. (Take, for example, the lives of Hitler and Napoleon.)

A person can become exhausted from contact with other people.

A remedy is for him to walk along a well-populated area noting people as he walks.

As he looks at more and more people...

...he will find he feels kinder toward them. Any feelings of overstrain with people can go away entirely.

Broad Application

This principle of extroversion and introversion could go much further in a society than it does. There is something that could be done by the government and by businesses in general which would probably eradicate the idea of strikes and would increase production quite markedly. Workers who strike are usually discontented, not so much with the conditions of work, but with work itself. They feel they are being victimized, they are being pressed into working at times when they do not want to work, and a strike comes as an actual relief. They can fight something. They can do something else than stand there and fiddle with a piece of machinery or account books. Dissatisfied workers are striking workers. If people become exhausted at work, if people are not content with work, if people are upset with work, they can be counted upon to find a sufficient number of grievances to strike. And, if management is given enough trouble and lack of cooperation on the part of the people on the lower chains of command, it can be certain that management sooner or later will create situations which cause workers to strike. In other words, bad conditions of work are actually not the reason for labor troubles and disputes. Weariness of work itself or an inability to control the area and environments of work *are* the actual cause of labor difficulties.

Any management given sufficient income to do so, if that management is not terribly irrational, will pay a decent working wage. And any workman given half a chance will perform his duties cheerfully. But once the environment itself becomes overstrained, once the company itself has become introverted by harmful acts on the part of the government, once the workers have been shown that they have no control over management, there can be, after that, labor disputes. Underlying all these obvious principles, however, are the principles of introversion and extroversion. Workers become so introverted at their tasks that they no longer are capable of affinity for their leaders and are no longer capable actually of viewing the environment in which they work. Therefore someone can come along and tell them that all the executives are ogres, which is obviously not true, and on the executive level someone can come along and tell the executives that all the workers are ogres, which is obviously, on that side, not true either.

In the absence of broad treatment on individuals, which is a gargantuan (enormous) task, a full program could be worked out that would handle the principle of introversion. It is certain that if workers or managers get introverted enough they will then find ways and means of inventing irrational games such as strikes, and so disrupt production and decent relationships and living conditions within the factory, the office or the concern.

The cure would be to extrovert workers on a very broad scale. This could be done, as one solution, by making it possible for all workers to have two jobs. It would be necessary for the company, or related interests such as the government, to make available a sufficient number of public works projects to provide work for workers outside the sphere of exact application. In other words, a man who is made to work continually inside and at a very fixed task would find a considerable relief at being able to go outside and work, particularly at some disrelated task. As an example, it would be a considerable relief to an accountant to be able to dig ditches for a while. A machinist running a stationary machine would actually find it a very joyful experience to push around a bulldozer.

Such a plan then would actually take introversion and extroversion with a large hand and bring it about. Workers who are working in fixed positions with their attention very close to them would then be permitted to look more widely and to handle things which tended to extrovert them. Such a program would be very ambitious but it would be found, it is certain, to result in better labor-management relations, better production and a considerable lessening of working and public tension on the subjects of jobs and pay.

In short, there are many things that could be done with the basic principle of extroversion–introversion. The principle is very simple: When an individual is made too introverted, things become less real in his surroundings and he has less affinity for them and cannot communicate with them well. In such a condition he becomes tired easily. Introversion results in weariness, exhaustion and then an inability to work. The remedy for it is extroversion, a good look at and communication with the wider environment, and unless this is practiced, then, in view of the fact that any worker is subject to injuries or illnesses of one kind or another, a dwindling spiral will ensue which makes work less and less palatable until at length it cannot be performed at all and we have the basis of not only a nonproductive, but a criminal society.

THE IMPORTANCE OF WORK

Work is the stable datum of this society. Without something to do there is nothing for which to live. A man who cannot work is as good as dead and usually prefers death and works to achieve it.

The mysteries of life are not today, with Scientology, very mysterious. Mystery is not a needful ingredient. Only the very irrational man desires to have vast secrets held away from him. Scientology has slashed through many of the complexities which have been erected for men and has bared the core of these problems. Scientology for the first time in man's history can predictably raise intelligence, increase ability, bring about a return of the ability to play a game, and permits man to escape from the dwindling spiral of his own disabilities. Therefore work itself can become again a pleasant and happy thing.

There is one thing which has been learned in Scientology which is very important to the state of mind of the workman. One very often feels in his society that he is working for the immediate paycheck and that he does not gain for the whole society anything of any importance. He does not know several things. One of these is how few good workmen are. On the level of executives, it is interesting to note how precious any large company finds a man really is who can handle and control jobs and men. Such people are rare. All the empty space in the structure of this workaday world is at the top.

And there is another thing which is quite important, and that is the fact that the world today has been led to believe, by mental philosophies calculated to betray it, that when one is dead it is all over and done with and that one has no further responsibility for anything. It is highly doubtful that this is true. One inherits tomorrow what he died out of yesterday.

Another thing we know is that men are not dispensable. It is a mechanism of old philosophies to tell men that if they think they are indispensable they should go down to the graveyard and take a look—those men were indispensable, too. This is the sheerest foolishness. If you really looked carefully in the graveyard, you would find the machinist who set the models going in yesteryear and without whom there would be no industry today. It is doubtful if such a feat is being performed just now.

A workman is not just a workman. A laborer is not just a laborer. An office worker is not just an office worker. They are living, breathing, important pillars on which the entire structure of our civilization is erected.

They are not cogs in a mighty machine.

They are the machine itself. ■

PRACTICAL EXERCISES

The following exercises will help you understand this booklet and increase your ability to actually apply the knowledge.

1 Think of an example of a confusion you have observed or experienced. Work out for yourself how the Doctrine of the Stable Datum could have been applied to that confusion.

2 Go out and find a confusion. Using the "Doctrine of the Stable Datum," handle that confusion.

3 Practice doing Reach and Withdraw. Drill giving the commands for Reach and Withdraw to a wall, naming a part of an object in the command, pointing and acknowledging each time. Refer to the procedure as needed while drilling. Drill the procedure until you can easily do Reach and Withdraw with no uncertainty.

4 Now, do Reach and Withdraw on another person on the tools of his job or his work environment.

5 Think of an example of bad control you have observed or experienced. Note why it was bad control.

6 Think of an example of good control you have observed or experienced. Note why it was good control.

7 Think of an example you have observed or experienced where an individual was not in good communication or familiar with a machine he was operating. Note his effectiveness on the job and the quality of what he was expected to produce.

8 Think of an example you have observed or experienced where an individual was in good communication or familiar with a machine he was operating. Note his effectiveness on the job and the quality of what he was expected to produce.

9 Take a walk around the block until you feel extroverted and more alert.

10 Find a person who is feeling exhaustion from work or who is upset from a domestic quarrel, etc., and have him or her take a walk until he or she feels extroverted.

RESULTS FROM APPLICATION

That Scientologists have and use technology that enables them to survive well in the workplace is reflected by the fact that more than 54 percent have positions as managers, artists, technicians, engineers, company owners or part owners, lawyers, or work in the medical profession.

But application of this data extends its effects well beyond the people who apply it—it is a positive influence on their environment and those around them, helping to create islands of sanity in the chaos of the workaday world as can be seen in the examples which follow.

Frequently exhausted after his daily endeavors, a man was shown what Mr. Hubbard had written about how to handle exhaustion.

"In the past, exhaustion always meant giving in and having to rest—and even rest didn't really handle the problem. The real reason for the exhaustion, and consequently the real solution, seemed to elude me. Exhaustion can be handled by doing just what Mr. Hubbard says. This is most important to me. Now I can remain fresh and alert throughout the day."

A musician receiving Reach and Withdraw on his area had considered that he was already in excellent communication with his environment. However, he was amazed at the change this simple action made in his operation.

"I had a great experience on this where I got a very clear concept of an ideal situation for creation of music and the level to which aesthetics can be raised. Only through Scientology could such an ideal be attained. What a simple and powerful piece of technology Reach and Withdraw is!"

Having learned the basic data on handling situations in the workplace, a man decided that he could do or be anything that he wanted to. So he chose to enter the catering field and promptly went out and got a position as a manager in a large catering firm that served more than 1,500 people at a new paper mill being built in South Africa.

"I had thirty-five or more staff and by applying to this job the basic Scientology I had studied, I was able to get them very productive. There were two shifts and four managers. My boss

SUCCESS IN THE WORKPLACE

Those who use Scientology in their careers have the tools to prosper and achieve their goals.

HOUSEHOLDS ABOVE THE POVERTY LINE

91%

66%

US Population   Scientologists

was always amazed at how smoothly my shift ran and how we were able to finish so quickly. At that time I realized the full effectiveness of this technology and its ability to change apparently hopeless situations for the better rather rapidly."

A young woman had been working long hours for many weeks, doing the same proofreading activity day after day. One day she found that this activity, which she normally had no trouble in doing, was getting harder and harder.

"Finally, near the end of the day, my sight gave out completely and I was unable to see at all for a few seconds. My eyes were hurting and things were a bit blurry. The person I was proofreading with knew the 'Take a Walk' remedy and took me outside and we went for a walk. At first I didn't want to look around because my eyes hurt, but she made me do it. After a little while my eyes stopped hurting and I was able to look around. I became cheerful again and was able to continue proofreading with no more strain."

A businesswoman was having difficulty in getting along with her boss. A friend referred her to some basic data from Mr. Hubbard on how to get along with others in the workaday world.

"Earlier this year, I had quite a lot of trouble in my firm. My boss constantly criticized me and complained to me about every petty detail in the office.

But it is completely different since I studied this data. Now when I am around he is not critical anymore and he even commends me. I know it is because of what I learned, as when I am not here, my colleagues still let him spoil their mood. But I can handle my whole environment now and for me, working conditions are very pleasant."

An executive in charge of personnel in a large southern California company had a serious problem coping with the number of people she had to deal with.

*"I had a long, long list of names of people who needed my attention and those people were constantly demanding my services. All the time I could have spent getting things done for them was being eaten up just fending off the demands. Somehow I could not get **anything** done. The larger this backlog became, the more overwhelmed I was. I decided to apply the 'Doctrine of the Stable Datum.' I looked at the ideal scene and started tackling each different job from the viewpoint of taking one job and completing it and then going on to the next. Total magic! At the end of the day I was cheerful and had a feeling of freedom. I knew that I had new undone jobs, but knew how to handle, so these were no longer a problem."*

Exhaustion would have been the expected result of one young woman's very heavy work schedule—if it weren't for her application of the technology of "Take a Walk."

"About four years ago I had a job as a physical education instructor in an elementary school. I worked from early in the morning till well into the afternoon, with class after class of very energetic youngsters.

"In the later part of the afternoon I worked as a translator, then went to a local gym where I conducted exercise classes until 10 in the evening.

"This was a very strenuous schedule to be on. I had 'every reason' to become exhausted, by most anyone's standards. But I never did, simply through application of the 'Take a Walk' technique. During breaks at school I would take a walk. Then I'd walk from the school to my translation job, putting my attention out on the environment as I went along. In short, every time I had a chance I would use this. People used to admire me for being in such shape that I could bear up to this schedule, but the real secret was the application of this technology."

A plumber from Georgia discovered Reach and Withdraw to be one of his most important working tools:

"I've done Reach and Withdraw many, many times, all with great success. One time my workshop was a confused mess, with parts and tools in disorder and lying about everywhere. I attributed this to heavy workload at that time. But upon starting some Reach and Withdraw I found, most unusually, that I couldn't seem to comfortably withdraw from the work space! I had gone into some sort of fixed idea about keeping up with the workload and had become very much stuck into the scene. When I spotted this inability to withdraw, I want you to know, I felt a great relief. The stuckness disappeared and I could once again get a rational view of things and put the shop into order."

Taking effective action to handle a fellow worker was a rewarding experience for a woman trained in Mr. Hubbard's technology.

"Quite a few years ago I was working at a company when a lady working there went into a nervous breakdown. At the time my bosses were concerned and didn't know what to do. I had a friend who was a Scientologist and seemed to know how to deal with such things, so I called her.

"She told me to take the person out for a walk and have her look at things in the environment. I walked into the office and said, 'I know what to do; I'll handle her.'

"I talked to the woman and told her I wanted to take her for a walk. I took her out and we began to walk, and I told her to look at different things as we went, just as my friend had said to. The woman soon started brightening up and told me to look at things, too! We continued and after a while she had come out of her difficulty altogether and was much happier. I was so pleased to be able to do something about the situation instead of just talking about it."

A German executive put in charge of a major production project faced a formidable confusion. The intricacy and sheer size of the undertaking were well beyond anything her group had attempted before, and they were not prepared to deal with it. She turned to one of Mr. Hubbard's basic tools for the workplace to accomplish the task.

"When I first reviewed the project description I was frankly dismayed. I didn't see how we could finish the job in the time we had. My personnel hadn't ever handled anything like this, and none of us had the training or experience needed to deal with some aspects of the work.

"To make matters worse, we had just finished another major project and were still recovering from the organizational strain it had involved.

"After swimming in the initial confusion of 'How on earth are we going to do this?' I realized that it **was** a confusion. An awfully simple realization, but my eyes were opened to the means to deal with the matter. I knew I first had to find a single stable datum. From there I would handle one thing, then another and another and somehow carry off the whole project.

"Resisting the feeling that I had to handle everything at once in a mad rush, I looked over some of the most important points that had to be solved to get the project rolling and chose one as the point to be settled first: who would be in charge of one particular phase of the production. Just doing this was a relief. At least there was one firm thing there I could concentrate on. I reviewed the possible personnel, named one for the job and briefed him on his responsibilities. Now I not only had one bit of the confusion out of the way, I also had someone to help me deal with the rest of it.

"Without going into all the details of what came after, we took one point at a time and handled it. How would these raw materials be gotten? Who would be in charge of this function and that? How were we going to make sure no 'loose ends' went by unnoticed and unhandled? And so on and so on, nailing down one detail after another, pushing forward actual production all the while. The confusion was under control and we were getting somewhere.

"It was by no means an easy job, and not without its share of shouting matches and near disasters. But we kept our sanity and managed to finish the project. We also gained new stable data from the experience which I'm sure will make future projects go a lot more smoothly."

GLOSSARY

acknowledge: give (someone) an acknowledgment. *See also* **acknowledgment** in this glossary.

acknowledgment: something said or done to inform another that his statement or action has been noted, understood and received.

affinity: love, liking or any other emotional attitude; the degree of liking. The basic definition of affinity is the consideration of distance, whether good or bad.

confront: to face without flinching or avoiding. The ability to confront is actually the ability to be there comfortably and perceive.

invalidate: refute, degrade, discredit or deny something someone else considers to be fact.

mass: the actual physical objects, the things of life.

Reach and Withdraw: a method of getting a person familiarized and in communication with things so that he can be more in control of them.

Scientology: an applied religious philosophy developed by L. Ron Hubbard. It is the study and handling of the spirit in relationship to itself, universes and other life. The word *Scientology* comes from the Latin *scio,* which means "know" and the Greek word *logos,* meaning "the word or outward form by which the inward thought is expressed and made known." Thus, Scientology means knowing about knowing.

win: an achievement toward accomplishing improvement in some area of a person's life. For example, a minor win would be a small improvement for a person, such as his experiencing an increased feeling of well-being. A major win would be a large improvement for the person such as a new awareness about some area of his life.

ABOUT L. RON HUBBARD

Born in Tilden, Nebraska on March 13, 1911, his road of discovery and dedication to his fellows began at an early age. By the age of nineteen, he had traveled more than a quarter of a million miles, examining the cultures of Java, Japan, India and the Philippines.

Returning to the United States in 1929, Ron resumed his formal education and studied mathematics, engineering and the then new field of nuclear physics—all providing vital tools for continued research. To finance that research, Ron embarked upon a literary career in the early 1930s, and soon became one of the most widely read authors of popular fiction. Yet never losing sight of his primary goal, he continued his mainline research through extensive travel and expeditions.

With the advent of World War II, he entered the United States Navy as a lieutenant (junior grade) and served as commander of antisubmarine corvettes. Left partially blind and lame from injuries sustained during combat, he was diagnosed as permanently disabled by 1945. Through application of his theories on the mind, however, he was not only able to help fellow servicemen, but also to regain his own health.

After five more years of intensive research, Ron's discoveries were presented to the world in *Dianetics: The Modern Science of Mental Health.* The first popular handbook on the human mind expressly written for the man in the street, *Dianetics* ushered in a new era of hope for mankind and a new phase of life for its author. He did, however, not cease his research, and as breakthrough after breakthrough was carefully codified through late 1951, the applied religious philosophy of Scientology was born.

Because Scientology explains the whole of life, there is no aspect of man's existence that L. Ron Hubbard's subsequent work did not address. Residing variously in the United States and England, his continued research brought forth solutions to such social ills as declining educational standards and pandemic drug abuse.

All told, L. Ron Hubbard's works on Scientology and Dianetics total forty million words of recorded lectures, books and writings. Together, these constitute the legacy of a lifetime that ended on January 24, 1986. Yet the passing of L. Ron Hubbard in no way constituted an end; for with a hundred million of his books in circulation and millions of people daily applying his technologies for betterment, it can truly be said the world still has no greater friend.

CHURCHES OF SCIENTOLOGY

WESTERN UNITED STATES

Church of Scientology of Arizona
2111 W. University Dr.
Mesa, Arizona 85201

Church of Scientology of the Valley
3619 West Magnolia Boulevard
Burbank, California 91506

Church of Scientology of Los Angeles
4810 Sunset Boulevard
Los Angeles, California 90027

Church of Scientology of Mountain View
2483 Old Middlefield Way
Mountain View, California 96043

Church of Scientology of Pasadena
263 E. Colorado Boulevard
Pasadena, California 91101

Church of Scientology of Sacramento
825 15th Street
Sacramento, California 95814

Church of Scientology of San Diego
635 "C" Street, Suite 200
San Diego, California 92101

Church of Scientology of San Francisco
83 McAllister Street
San Francisco, California 94102

Church of Scientology of Stevens Creek
80 E. Rosemary
San Jose, California 95112

Church of Scientology of Santa Barbara
524 State Street
Santa Barbara, California 93101

Church of Scientology of Orange County
1451 Irvine Boulevard
Tustin, California 92680

Church of Scientology of Colorado
375 S. Navajo Street
Denver, Colorado 80223

Church of Scientology of Hawaii
1146 Bethel Street
Honolulu, Hawaii 96813

Church of Scientology of Minnesota
Twin Cities
1011 Nicollet Mall
Minneapolis, Minnesota 55403

Church of Scientology of Kansas City
3619 Broadway
Kansas City, Missouri 64111

Church of Scientology of Missouri
9510 Page Boulevard
St. Louis, Missouri 63132

Church of Scientology of Nevada
846 E. Sahara Avenue
Las Vegas, Nevada 89104

Church of Scientology of New Mexico
8106 Menaul Boulevard N.E.
Albuquerque, New Mexico 87110

Church of Scientology of Portland
323 S.W. Washington
Portland, Oregon 97204

Church of Scientology of Texas
2200 Guadalupe
Austin, Texas 78705

Church of Scientology of Utah
1931 S. 1100 East
Salt Lake City, Utah 84106

Church of Scientology of Washington State
2226 3rd Avenue
Seattle, Washington 98121

EASTERN UNITED STATES

Church of Scientology of Connecticut
909 Whalley Avenue
New Haven, Connecticut 06515

Church of Scientology of Florida
120 Giralda Avenue
Coral Gables, Florida 33134

Church of Scientology of Orlando
1830 East Colonial Drive
Orlando, Florida 32803

Church of Scientology of Tampa
3617 Henderson Boulevard
Tampa, Florida 33609

Church of Scientology of Georgia
2632 Piedmont Road, N.E.
Atlanta, Georgia 30324

Church of Scientology of Illinois
3011 N. Lincoln Avenue
Chicago, Illinois 60657

Church of Scientology of Boston
448 Beacon Street
Boston, Massachusetts 02115

Church of Scientology of Ann Arbor
2355 West Stadium Boulevard
Ann Arbor, Michigan 48103

Church of Scientology of Michigan
321 Williams Street
Royal Oak, Michigan 48067

Church of Scientology of Buffalo
47 West Huron Street
Buffalo, New York 14202

Church of Scientology of Long Island
99 Railroad Station Plaza
Hicksville, New York 11801

Church of Scientology of New York
227 West 46th Street
New York City, New York 10036

Church of Scientology of Cincinnati
215 West 4th Street, 5th Floor
Cincinnati, Ohio 45202

Church of Scientology of Ohio
30 North High Street
Columbus, Ohio 43215

Church of Scientology of Pennsylvania
1315 Race Street
Philadelphia, Pennsylvania 19107

Founding Church of Scientology of Washington, DC
2125 "S" Street N.W.
Washington, DC 20008

PUERTO RICO

Church of Scientology of Puerto Rico
272 JT Piniero Avenue
Hyde Park, Hato Rey
Puerto Rico 00918

UNITED KINGDOM

Church of Scientology of Birmingham
Albert House, 3rd Floor
24 Albert Street
Birmingham
England B4 7UD

Church of Scientology of Brighton
5 St. Georges Place
London Road
Brighton, Sussex
England BN1 4GA

Church of Scientology Saint Hill Foundation
Saint Hill Manor
East Grinstead, West Sussex
England RH19 4JY

Church of Scientology of London
68 Tottenham Court Road
London
England W1P 0BB

Church of Scientology of Manchester
258 Deansgate
Manchester
England M3 4BG

Church of Scientology of Plymouth
41 Ebrington Street
Plymouth, Devon
England PL4 9AA

Church of Scientology of Sunderland
51 Fawcett Street
Sunderland, Tyne and Wear
England SR1 1RS

Hubbard Academy of Personal Independence
20 Southbridge
Edinburgh
Scotland EH1 1LL

EUROPE

Austria

Church of Scientology of Austria
Schottenfeldgasse 13/15
1070 Wien

Belgium

Church of Scientology of Belgium
61, rue du Prince Royal
1050 Bruxelles

Denmark

Church of Scientology of Jylland
Guldsmedegade 17, 2
8000 Aarhus C

Church of Scientology of Copenhagen
Store Kongensgade 55
1264 Copenhagen K

Church of Scientology of Denmark
Gammel Kongevej 3–5, 1
1610 Copenhagen V

France

Church of Scientology of Angers
10–12, rue Max Richard
49100 Angers

Church of Scientology of Clermont-Ferrand
1, rue Ballainvilliers
63000 Clermont-Ferrand

Church of Scientology of Lyon
3, place des Capucins
69001 Lyon

Church of Scientology of Paris
65, rue de Dunkerque
75009 Paris

Church of Scientology of Saint-Étienne
24, rue Marengo
42000 Saint-Étienne

Germany

Church of Scientology of Berlin
Sponholzstraße 51–52
12159 Berlin

Church of Scientology of Düsseldorf
Friedrichstraße 28
40217 Düsseldorf

Church of Scientology of Frankfurt
Darmstädter Landstraße 213
60598 Frankfurt

Church of Scientology of Hamburg
Steindamm 63
20099 Hamburg

Church of Scientology of Hanover
Hubertusstraße 2
30163 Hannover

Church of Scientology of Munich
Beichstraße 12
80802 München

Church of Scientology of Stuttgart
Urbanstraße 70
70182 Stuttgart

Israel

Dianetics and Scientology College of Israel
42 Gorden Street, 2nd Floor
Tel Aviv 66023

Italy

Church of Scientology of Brescia
Via Fratelli Bronzetti, 20
25125 Brescia

Church of Scientology of Catania
Via Garibaldi, 9
95121 Catania

Church of Scientology of Milan
Via Abetone, 10
20137 Milano

Church of Scientology of Monza
Via Cavour, 5
20052 Monza

Church of Scientology of Novara
Corso Cavallotti, 7
28100 Novara

Church of Scientology of Nuoro
Via Lamarmora, 115
08100 Nuoro

Church of Scientology of Padua
Via Mameli, 1/5
35131 Padova

Church of Scientology of Pordenone
Via Montereale, 10/C
33170 Pordenone

Church of Scientology of Rome
Via della Pineta Sacchetti, 201
00185 Roma

Church of Scientology of Turin
Via Bersezio, 7
10152 Torino

Church of Scientology of Verona
Via Vicolo Chiodo, 4/A
37121 Verona

Netherlands

Church of Scientology of Amsterdam
Nieuwe Zijds Voorburgwal 271
1012 RL Amsterdam

Norway

Church of Scientology of Norway
Storgata 9
0155 Oslo 1

Portugal

Church of Scientology of Portugal
Rua Actor Taborda 39–5°
1000 Lisboa

Russia

Hubbard Humanitarian Center
103064 Moscow
Homutovskiy Tupik 7, Russia

Spain

Dianetics Civil Association of Barcelona
C/ Pau Clarís 85, Principal dcha.
08010 Barcelona

Dianetics Civil Association of Madrid
C/ Montera 20, 1° dcha.
28013 Madrid

Sweden

Church of Scientology of Göteborg
Odinsgatan 8, 2 tr.
411 03 Göteborg

Church of Scientology of Malmö
Lantmannagatan 62 C
214 48 Malmö

Church of Scientology of Stockholm
St. Eriksgatan 56
112 34 Stockholm

Switzerland

Church of Scientology of Basel
Herrengrabenweg 56
4054 Basel

Church of Scientology of Bern
Dammweg 29
Postfach 352
3000 Bern 11

Church of Scientology of Geneva
Route de Saint-Julien 7–9 C.P. 823
1227 Carouge, Genève

Church of Scientology of Lausanne
10, rue de la Madeleine
1003 Lausanne

Church of Scientology of Zurich
Badenerstrasse 141
8004 Zürich

AFRICA

Church of Scientology of Cape Town
St. Georges Centre, 2nd Floor
13 Hout Street
Cape Town 8001
Republic of South Africa

Church of Scientology of Durban
57 College Lane
Durban 4001
Republic of South Africa

Church of Scientology of Johannesburg
Security Building, 2nd Floor
95 Commissioner Street
Johannesburg 2001
Republic of South Africa

Church of Scientology of Johannesburg North
1st Floor Bordeaux Centre
Gordon and Jan Smuts Ave.
Bordeaux, Randburg 2125
Republic of South Africa

Church of Scientology of Port Elizabeth
2 St. Christopher Place
27 Westbourne Road Central
Port Elizabeth 6001
Republic of South Africa

Church of Scientology of Pretoria
306 Ancore Building
Jeppe and Esselen Streets
Pretoria 0002
Republic of South Africa

Church of Scientology of Bulawayo
Southampton House, Suite 202
Main Street and 9th Avenue
Bulawayo, Zimbabwe

Church of Scientology of Harare
PO Box 3524
87 Livingston Road
Harare, Zimbabwe

AUSTRALIA, NEW ZEALAND AND OCEANIA

Australia

Church of Scientology of Adelaide
24–28 Waymouth Street
Adelaide, South Australia 5000

Church of Scientology of Brisbane
106 Edward Street
Brisbane, Queensland 4000

Church of Scientology of Australian Capital Territory
108 Bunda Street, Suite 16
Civic Canberra, A.C.T. 2601

Church of Scientology of Melbourne
42–44 Russell Street
Melbourne, Victoria 3000

Church of Scientology of Perth
39–41 King Street
Perth, Western Australia 6000

Church of Scientology of Sydney
201 Castlereagh Street
Sydney, New South Wales 2000

Japan

Scientology Tokyo
1-23-1 Higashi Gotanda
Shinagawa-ku
Tokyo, Japan 141

New Zealand

Church of Scientology New Zealand
32 Lorne Street
Auckland 1

LATIN AMERICA

Colombia

Dianetics Cultural Center
Calle 95 No. 19-A-28
Barrio Chico, Bogotá

Mexico

Dianetics Cultural Organization, A.C.
Pedro Moreno 1078 Int 3
Sector Juárez, Guadalajara, Jalisco

Dianetics Cultural Association, A.C.
Carrillo Puerto 54 Bis
Colonia Coyoacán
C.P. 04000, Mexico, D.F.

Latin American Cultural Center, A.C.
Durango 105
Colonia Roma
C.P. 03100, Mexico, D.F.

Institute of Applied Philosophy, A.C.
Juan de Dios Arias 83
Colonia Vista Alegre
Mexico, D.F.

Dianetics Technological Institute, A.C.
Avenida Juan Escutia 29
Colonia Condesa
Delegación Cuauhtemoc
C.P. 06140, Mexico, D.F.

Dianetics Development Organization, A.C.
Heriberto Frías 420
Colonia Narvarte
C.P. 03020, Mexico, D.F.

Dianetics Cultural Organization, A.C.
Nicolás San Juan 1734
Colonia del Valle
C.P. 03100, Mexico, D.F.

Venezuela

Dianetics Cultural Organization, A.C.
Avenida Principal de las Palmas,
Cruce Con Calle Carúpano
Quinta Suha, Las Palmas
Caracas

Dianetics Cultural Association, A.C.
Avenida 101, 150-23
Urbanización La Alegría
Apartado Postal 833
Valencia

CANADA

Church of Scientology of Edmonton
10187 112th Street
Edmonton, Alberta
Canada T5K 1M1

Church of Scientology of Kitchener
104 King Street West
Kitchener, Ontario
Canada N2G 2K6

Church of Scientology of Montreal
4489 Papineau Street
Montréal, Québec
Canada H2H 1T7

Church of Scientology of Ottawa
150 Rideau Street, 2nd Floor
Ottawa, Ontario
Canada K1N 5X6

Church of Scientology of Quebec
350 Bd Chareste Est
Québec, Québec
Canada G1K 3H5

Church of Scientology of Toronto
696 Yonge Street, 2nd Floor
Toronto, Ontario
Canada M4Y 2A7

Church of Scientology of Vancouver
401 West Hasting Street
Vancouver, British Columbia
Canada V6B 1L5

Church of Scientology of Winnipeg
388 Donald Street, Suite 125
Winnipeg, Manitoba
Canada R3B 2J4

CELEBRITY CENTRES

**Church of Scientology
Celebrity Centre International**
5930 Franklin Avenue
Hollywood, California 90028

**Church of Scientology
Celebrity Centre Dallas**
10500 Steppington Drive, Suite 100
Dallas, Texas 75230

Bridge Publications, Inc.
4751 Fountain Ave., Los Angeles, CA 90029
ISBN 0-88404-922-1
NEW ERA Publications International ApS
Store Kongensgade 55, 1264 Copenhagen K, Denmark
ISBN 87-7816-119-3

An L. RON HUBBARD Publication

**Church of Scientology
Celebrity Centre Las Vegas**
1100 South 10th Street
Las Vegas, Nevada 89104

**Church of Scientology
Celebrity Centre Nashville**
38 Music Square West
Nashville, Tennessee 37203

**Church of Scientology
Celebrity Centre New York**
65 East 82nd Street
New York City, New York 10036

**Church of Scientology
Celebrity Centre Portland**
709 Southwest Salmon Street
Portland, Oregon 97205

**Church of Scientology
Celebrity Centre Washington, DC**
4214 16th Street N.W.
Washington, DC 20011

**Church of Scientology
Celebrity Centre London**
27 Westbourne Grove
London W2, England

**Church of Scientology
Celebrity Centre Vienna**
Senefeldergasse 11/5
1100 Wien, Austria

**Church of Scientology
Celebrity Centre Paris**
69, rue Legendre
75017 Paris, France

**Church of Scientology
Celebrity Centre Düsseldorf**
Grupellostraße 28
40210 Düsseldorf, Germany

**Church of Scientology
Celebrity Centre Hamburg**
Eppendorfer Landstraße 35
20249 Hamburg, Germany

**Church of Scientology
Celebrity Centre Munich**
Landshuter Allee 42
80637 München, Germany

SCIENTOLOGY MISSIONS

Scientology Missions International
6331 Hollywood Boulevard,
Suite 501
Los Angeles, California 90028

▲ Scientology Missions International
Expansion Office
210 South Fort Harrison Avenue
Clearwater, Florida 34616

Western United States

▲ Scientology Missions International
Western United States Office
1307 N. New Hampshire,
Suite 101
Los Angeles, California 90027

Eastern United States

▲ Scientology Missions International
Eastern United States Office
349 W. 48th Street
New York City, New York 10036

United Kingdom

▲ Scientology Missions International
United Kingdom Office
Saint Hill Manor
East Grinstead, West Sussex
England RH19 4JY

Europe

▲ Scientology Missions International
European Office
Store Kongensgade 55
1264 Copenhagen K
Denmark

Africa

▲ Scientology Missions International
African Office
Security Building, 2nd Floor
95 Commissioner Street
Johannesburg 2001
Republic of South Africa

Australia, New Zealand and Oceania

▲ Scientology Missions International
Australian, New Zealand and
Oceanian Office
201 Castlereagh Street
Sydney, New South Wales 2000
Australia

Latin America

▲ Scientology Missions International
Latin American Office
Federación Mexicana de
Dianética
Pomona 53
Colonia Roma
C.P. 06700, Mexico, D.F.

Canada

▲ Scientology Missions International
Canadian Office
696 Yonge Street
Toronto, Ontario
Canada M4Y 2A7

INTERNATIONAL HUBBARD ECCLESIASTICAL LEAGUE OF PASTORS

International Office
6331 Hollywood Boulevard, Suite 901
Los Angeles, California 90028
Telephone: 213-960-3560
US & Canada: 1-800-HELP-4-YU

Western United States
▲ Continental Liaison Office
Western United States
1307 N. New Hampshire
Los Angeles, California 90027

Eastern United States
▲ Continental Liaison Office
Eastern United States
349 W. 48th Street
New York City, New York 10036

United Kingdom
▲ Continental Liaison Office
United Kingdom
Saint Hill Manor
East Grinstead, West Sussex
England RH19 4JY

Canada
▲ Continental Liaison Office Canada
696 Yonge Street
Toronto, Ontario
Canada M4Y 2A7

Africa
▲ Continental Liaison Office Africa
Security Building, 4th Floor
95 Commissioner Street
Johannesburg 2001
Republic of South Africa

Latin America
▲ Continental Liaison Office
Latin America
Federación Mexicana de Dianética
Avenida Montevideo 486
Colonia Linda Vista
C.P. 07300
Mexico, D.F.

Australia, New Zealand and Oceania
▲ Continental Liaison Office ANZO
201 Castlereagh Street, 3rd Floor
Sydney, New South Wales 2000
Australia

Europe
▲ Continental Liaison Office Europe
Store Kongensgade 55
1264 Copenhagen K
Denmark